P'HOWA COMMENTARY

P'howa Commentary

INSTRUCTIONS FOR
THE PRACTICE OF
CONSCIOUSNESS TRANSFERENCE
AS REVEALED BY
RIGDZIN LONGSAL NYINGPO

Chagdud Khadro

PADMA PUBLISHING
1998

Published by
Padma Publishing
P.O. Box 279
Junction City, CA 96048

© Padma Publishing 1998

ISBN 1-881847-10-1

Printed in the United States

Contents

CONTENTS

Foreword

THE PRACTICE OF P'HOWA, the transference of consciousness at the moment of death, has been one of my primary means of benefiting others since I was a child. In this life and indeed—from the stories I have heard—in my preceding lifetime, I seem to have had the power to accomplish p'howa.

When I left Tibet in exile in 1959, I realized that competence in p'howa would be extremely useful for my fellow refugees, faced as they were with aggression, deprivation, and unfamiliar conditions. I began to teach the practice widely.

In Nepal in 1978, when I taught the practice to a group of Western dharma students for the first time, my future wife, now known as Chagdud Khadro, was among them. She attained signs of accomplishment rather easily, and over the years she showed more and more interest in the practice. In 1986, on the basis of clear indications that arose in meditation, I authorized her to teach, and in 1997 I authorized her to give the necessary Amitabha empowerment. I feel confident she will not lead others astray, and I have seen that those who practice with her achieve signs of successful practice. I hope that this compilation of teachings will enhance the confidence of those who have received p'howa instruction. I pray that they will find liberation into the pure realm of Dewachen at the moment of death.

Chagdud Tulku
Chagdud Khadro Ling
Três Coroas, Brazil

Preface

THIS P'HOWA BOOK has been written as a manual for those who have received teachings and training from a qualified p'howa teacher. It has not been written for the general dharma readership, and does not include the wealth of stories and personal insights that have enriched the oral transmission of His Eminence Chagdud Tulku Rinpoche over the years. Nor is this a scholarly presentation, for I do not have the slightest pretense of being a scholar, either by Tibetan criteria, which are very exacting indeed, or by Western standards. This book is merely a reference, a reminder of essential points covered in the oral teachings.

Nevertheless, as short as the book is, it has taken a surprisingly long time to write, for p'howa incorporates all the fundamentals of Vajrayana development and completion stage practice and brings about profound insight into the workings of mind, speech, and body. Being a practitioner of limited acuity, it has taken me quite a while to be able to draw on a depth of experience that would produce a useful work. I am totally grateful to Chagdud Rinpoche for teaching me p'howa twenty years ago in Nepal, for encouraging me to compile his teachings, and for authorizing me to teach. Rinpoche has many manifestations, both peaceful and wrathful, but at the core lies almost infinite patience, with me, with sentient beings. Without his willingness to teach me, again and again correcting and expanding my practice, I surely would not be able to teach and guide others in the accomplishment of p'howa.

It has also been a great privilege—and responsibility—to work with a hidden treasure text (Tib. *terma*) of Rigdzin Longsal Nyingpo, long a dharma hero of mine. Born in 1685, prophesied as a great lama, by the age of seven he had mastered reading and writing and insisted that he wanted to be a monk. He was prevented from taking ordination by his father until, at twenty, he ran away to Katog Gonpa. There he trained under Dempa Konchog Gyaltsen and received Great Perfection (Dzogchen) transmission, directly recognizing his own absolute nature. An extremely diligent practitioner, who allowed no hardships to interfere with his retreats, he was revered by the dharma protectors, who became his servants, and he was tested by the local deities, whom he tamed. Although he had a peaceful demeanor, he was feared by demons, whom he overwhelmed by miraculous powers.

At twenty-eight he left the monastery and practiced in solitary, dangerous places. Soon after, he met Düdül Dorje, his main teacher, who received him just as would a father being reunited with his son. Düdül Dorje told him, "You have hidden treasure texts to reveal," and offered him advice. Once more Longsal Nyingpo entered retreat. A few years later, when he was thirty-two, Guru Padmasambhava, dressed as a yogi, approached him and gave him an index of treasure texts to reveal. He continued his retreat until his realization had fully ripened.

This would be the pattern throughout his life, to perfect accomplishment in retreat. After revealing each of his treasure texts, he entered retreat to ensure that every aspect of the practice was completely brought forth and to establish a powerful foundation for practitioners who would follow him. Nothing that he could achieve by effort did he leave to chance. This, as much as his qualities as a revealer of hidden treasure texts and as a siddha, made him a heroic practitioner.

The time came when it was appropriate for Longsal Nyingpo to reveal the hidden treasure text of a practice related to the wrathful form of Guru Rinpoche. The treasure was located near a monastery of a different tradition, whose residents were at least skeptical about, and probably hostile to, a Nyingmapa treasure text being revealed in their vicinity. When Longsal Nyingpo sent a message requesting the monastery's cooperation in revealing the treasure, the monks conspired to thwart him. Thus, when Longsal Nyingpo rode up to the monastery, he encountered prayer flags dyed black instead of the usual array of colors. Instead of fragrant cedar incense, the acrid smell of *gugul,* used to banish demons, filled the air. Instead of auspicious prayers, the monks rumbled wrathful incantations. He dismounted, they led him to a throne draped in black, and Longsal Nyingpo thought how perfect the signs were. Not knowing that the treasure text to be revealed was Wrathful Guru Rinpoche, the monks had inadvertently created the best possible interdependence for the fulfillment of wrathful activity.

One day, while Longsal Nyingpo was traveling in Tromtar, the region of Chagdud Rinpoche's birth, a man offered him a fine copper pot. His wife, who was very fond of the pot, inwardly regretted the offering. Longsal Nyingpo, seeing her thoughts, took a horse hair and cut the pot precisely into two halves, and accepted only one as an offering.

The presence of this saintly being created auspiciousness for those around him. His horse left a footprint in rock, and when it died and was cremated, relics were found in the ashes. Similarly, when his yak died, images were visible on its bones.

Rigdzin Longsal Nyingpo's dharma legacy was superb. Along with his teacher, Düdül Dorje, he increased the enlightened activity at Katog Gonpa. Particularly at the end of his life, he focused his tremendous capabilities on the strengthening of Katog. His foremost student was his own son, Sonam Detsen, the reincarnation of Düdül Dorje. The Longsal lineage remains one of the primary lineages practiced at Chagdud Gonpa in Kham, Eastern Tibet.

Longsal Nyingpo died at the age of sixty-eight, amid many miraculous signs, and extraordinary relics were discovered in his cremation ashes.

The blessings of Rigdzin Longsal Nyingpo's p'howa treasure text remain undiminished and are clearly evident in the lives—and deaths—of practitioners today. The people listed below showed clear signs of p'howa accomplishment. All of them led lives of ordinary householders, and for several of them p'howa was their only connection to Tibetan Buddhism, but of the countless beings in the endless cycles of samsara, they found liberation into the pure realm of Dewachen. There they have manifested as bodhisattvas, and nothing will hinder their attainment of ultimate enlightenment.

Alice Miranda, a Canadian woman, died of breast cancer. Her p'howa practice was supported by Helen Orr.

Terri Laska died of lung cancer. She was supported by members of the Chagdud Gonpa sangha in the moment after her death.

Reece Smith died of colon cancer. After receiving p'howa teachings from Chagdud Rinpoche in 1981, he practiced regularly. At the moment before his death in 1996, he simply said, "*P'hat, p'hat, p'hat,*" transferring his consciousness with excellent signs. Sangha member Jeannie Chapman was among those who supported his final p'howa.

Premal Gold came to Chagdud Rinpoche after being diagnosed with breast cancer. Though she had been practicing in a non-Buddhist tradition, she had faith in the method of p'howa and practiced diligently for the short time remaining to her. Supported by members of the Chagdud Gonpa sangha at the moment of her death, she died with clear signs.

Neilly Joe Gracia, an eight-year-old sangha member, died in 1994 of brain cancer at Rigdzin Ling, Chagdud Rinpoche's North American seat. He was surrounded by sangha members and supported immediately after his death by Chagdud Rinpoche, who was in Moscow at the time. After several phone calls and uncertainty about the signs, Rinpoche finally said, "I know his consciousness has been transferred," and gave explicit instructions for detecting the signs. The signs were just as he explained.

Carmen Gomez died in Rio de Janeiro in 1995 of heart disease, supported by her daughter, Clarita Maia, and by Chagdud Rinpoche. Although she was not a practitioner, she showed definite signs of transference.

The support of sangha members trained in p'howa is invaluable at the moment of death. One of my aspirations in writing this book and in training people in transference is the creation of more p'howa support groups made up of people who train together and make a commitment to serve whoever among them enters the transition of dying. Such groups have been established in the United States, Brazil, Uruguay, and Australia, but there still exists much untapped potential. I have been inspired by the compassion of participants in p'howa training and their willingness to attend to the dying. This book fulfills a promise I made to many of them. I hope to do much more. And, deeply, I hope that they and all who have a connection to the profound path of p'howa will find liberation into the pure realm of Buddha Amitabha and ultimate enlightenment.

P'HOWA COMMENTARY

P'howa: Toward Mastery in Life, Death, and Rebirth

TRAINING IN P'HOWA, transference of consciousness at the moment of death, inspires confidence in one's life, in one's spiritual practice, and in one's dying. In daily life, even the most ordinary activities take on new significance when viewed through the lens of impermanence and death. The p'howa teachings directly address the fact that death is inevitable and that with each moment one moves closer to death. Clinging to fictitious stability will not prevent or even slow this inexorable movement toward death. Confidence comes from using whatever arises within the play of impermanence as an opportunity to purify obscurations and mental poisons, and to generate merit. Confidence also comes from direct recognition of what is unchanging, authentic, and absolute, and being able to experience this again and again. The teachings and training of p'howa lead to assurance of conduct within relative reality and assurance arising from recognizing the absolute nature of reality. Cutting through the denial of death allows one to clearly see the importance of one's human existence.

The ability to perform p'howa ensures that even if death intervenes and cuts short one's opportunity to practice in this lifetime, one will be able to continue the path amid superb conditions. Even with unpurified karma, the practitioner need not fall back into the confusion and waywardness of samsara. Moreover, p'howa provides excellent training in the development and completion stages of Vajrayana Buddhism, incorporating aspects of the three higher approaches—maha-, anu-, and atiyoga. Training well in p'howa thus establishes a strong basis for learning other Vajrayana practices and for achieving the special signs of Vajrayana accomplishment.

P'howa training instills confidence in terms of dying and the moment of death by providing the practitioner with the means to liberate his or her consciousness into Buddha Amitabha's pure realm of Dewachen (Great Bliss), or at least to attain a high rebirth that will be conducive to spiritual practice. In the practice known as the "p'howa of the three recognitions," the central channel is recognized as the path, the consciousness sphere as the traveler on the path, and the heart-mind of Buddha Amitabha as the destination. In the course of training, actual physical signs arise, indicating that a small opening has appeared in the crown chakra and the path will be available for transference at the time of death. These signs usually occur within a day or two when one trains in the presence of a p'howa master, within a week or two if one practices alone. Training thereafter makes p'howa almost an automatic reflex, giving practitioners confidence that, even in adverse circumstances, they could remember and accomplish transference.

The p'howa of the three recognitions is the fourth of five categories of p'howa and comes from many lineages. Three categories correspond directly to the three kayas. Dharmakaya p'howa is transference into a state of unimpeded, timeless awareness (Tib. *yeshe*)—into basic space, emptiness. Sambhogakaya p'howa is transference into a state of sheer lucidity, nondual perception of pure appearance that arises continuously from emptiness. Nirmanakaya p'howa is transference into a state of all-pervasive compassion. The p'howa of the three recognitions is related to nirmanakaya transference, in that one transfers consciousness into the nirmanakaya manifestation of Buddha Amitabha's compassion, the pure realm of Dewachen.

Dharmakaya, sambhogakaya, and nirmanakaya p'howa can be accomplished in the corresponding afterdeath intermediate states (Tib. *bardo*) or through meditative techniques in one's lifetime. This will be explained more fully in the chapter on accomplishing p'howa at the time of death.The fifth category, the "p'howa of the compassionate hook," involves transferring the consciousness of another person. This will be explained in the same chapter.

The p'howa of the three recognitions involves aspects of maha-, anu-, and atiyoga and requires good visualization. One must also develop the ability to momentarily relax one's focus on the images of visualization, rest the mind in the nondual experience of the insepa-rability of one's consciousness and the aware-ness of Buddha Amitabha, then to bring forth the visualization again. P'howa thus serves as an excellent training for the development and completion stages of Vajrayana practice.

As ordinary beings, we are bound by the limiting sense of our body as a real, solid entity. But even a moment's reflection reminds us that the body constantly changes, from the time of birth to the moment of death. We cannot find even a microsecond of stability, not a shred of inherent existence, of anything more than an in-terdependent coalescence of elements and func-tions that we label our "body" for the duration of this lifetime bardo. After death, when the body is no longer animated by consciousness, any semblance of a physical entity dissolves.

Besides form, we are bound by feelings, per-ceptions, volition (impulses), and consciousness, which together constitute the five aggregates that hinder unimpeded awareness. When, through contemplation of impermanence and meditative insight we begin to recognize the empty nature of the aggregates, we also begin to slip free of the delusion imposed by them. Through Vajrayana's transformative methods of development stage practice, especially deity visualization, we begin to directly experience the pure display of the deity's enlightened body, speech, and mind.

Ultimately, our Vajrayana commitment requires us to recognize that all that arises as form, inseparable from its own empty nature, is the display of the deity's form. All that arises as sound, inseparable from emptiness, is the sound of the deity's mantra. All that arises as mental phenomena, in essence empty, is the display of the deity's mind. Maintaining this pure perspective at the time of dying—when the body is decaying, when sounds fade into confusion, when concepts and emotions tend to spin out of control—poses a tremendous challenge. We cannot really expect to succeed unless we have practiced thoroughly in this lifetime, cutting through the attachments and aversions that bind us to delusion and obscure the pure essence of all phenomena.

By becoming clearly cognizant of death's imminence and utilizing extraordinary Vajrayana meditation techniques, p'howa practitioners increase their chances of negotiating the transition of dying with some measure of equanimity and compassion, and of transferring directly from this life into Buddha Amitabha's pure realm. With authentic mastery of p'howa, one no longer needs favorable outward circumstances to die well. Instead, the inner recognition of everything as display, intrinsically pure, allows peace and at-oneness with the dreamlike illusion of dying and, when the moment ripens, provides a trajectory into a state free of samsaric illusion.

The Four Causes of Rebirth
in Buddha Amitabha's
Pure Realm of Dewachen

ACCORDING TO THE SUTRA known as the *Rolling of Drums,* countless eons ago there was a joyous kingdom whose sovereign had great devotion for the buddha of that time, Lokeshvaraja. The king renounced his kingdom, became a monk, and vowed to reach enlightenment. He expressed his bodhichitta intention through forty-eight vows, and promised to refuse buddhahood if any of these vows were not fulfilled. With these words, the earth trembled and flowers rained down from the skies. Praises resounded and with them the prophecy that this monk would surely become a buddha. And so he did, as the Buddha Amitabha.

In his lifetime as this bodhisattva monk, Amitabha saw that countless pure realms existed for realized ones who had been victorious over the mind's delusions, but no such realm was accessible to those still struggling on the path. Among his forty-eight vows was the aspiration to create a pure realm for all those who heard his name, wished to attain that realm, established the roots of virtue, and dedicated their merit in order to be reborn there. So powerful was his intention that he swore to refuse buddhahood if it did not enable him to manifest such a realm.

In his enlightened state, Buddha Amitabha remains in unimpeded awareness of dharmakaya, in uninterrupted recognition of absolute nature, in all-encompassing spaciousness. But the empty nature, the basic space, of dharmakaya is not mere voidness; rather it holds the full potential to arise unceasingly as the appearances of sambhogakaya and nirmanakaya. The sambhogakaya pure realms and celestial mansions manifest to buddhas and tenth-level bodhisattvas, who have removed their obscurations and thus can experience and enjoy such pure phenomena. Nirmanakaya appearances arise according to the karma of the beings of the six realms.

Dewachen, the realm of "Great Bliss" that

manifested as a result of Buddha Amitabha's aspirations, can be attained by beings who have not yet become tenth-level bodhisattvas but who have faith in Amitabha and aspire to be reborn in his pure realm. There they can continue their path to enlightenment in a blissful environment, beyond the reach of suffering. In Vajrayana Buddhism, directing one's rebirth to Dewachen is most effectively accomplished by means of p'howa.

Even someone who has not achieved a high degree of purification can, through strong faith and aspiration, be reborn in Dewachen. After death, such a person's consciousness is enveloped by a lotus until most obscurations dissolve and the pure realm becomes perceptible. When the lotus opens, one experiences a land of harmonious elements, devoid of friction, with nothing jagged, dangerous, or harmful. The temperature itself adjusts to individual preferences. Flowers carpet the ground and the wind blows lightly, carrying delightful fragrances. A wondrous variety of birds sing the melodious songs of dharma, bells ring sweetly, and the merest vibration of trees carries sacred meaning.

The resplendent palace of Buddha Amitabha stands in the center of Dewachen and within it sits the Buddha himself, on a magnificent throne supported by eight peacocks. To behold the face of Amitabha purifies many obscurations, to receive teachings directly from him opens countless doors of meditative concentration. One can receive dharma teachings and visit other pure realms according to one's wishes.

Behind the palace grows a magnificent bodhi tree that has a mantra on every leaf and is laden with jewels. To see this tree protects sight, to touch it ensures good health, and to think about it brings wonderful concentration.

The beings in Dewachen have golden bodies, and as they near enlightenment the thirty-two major and eighty minor marks of enlightened form appear. The members of the noble sangha are monks, like Amitabha himself, but many other manifestations of wisdom beings also abide there.

No stress, boredom, negativity, or suffering mars the perfection of Dewachen, yet one is not isolated from the conditions of beings caught in the cycles of samsara. One can witness their plight and know simultaneously their relative pain and their ultimately illusory nature. Because one's compassion as a full-fledged bodhisattva is unobstructed, one can choose to emanate and take rebirth in samsara, not out of karmic necessity but out of love for and commitment to other beings. To know these wondrous qualities of Dewachen and to aspire to rebirth there is the first of four causes of finding such a rebirth.

The second cause is pure motivation: out of compassion for beings, we seek enlightenment in order to bring them likewise to enlightenment. This awakening of bodhichitta occurs when the pure qualities of our own buddha nature—compassion, love, joy, and equanimity—surge through the layers of ordinary self-centered concerns and arouse our spirituality. In terms of p'howa, it means that we intend to accomplish this practice and to use it as a means of liberating ourselves from the limitations of samsara in order to benefit others. Therefore, we are willing to make the effort to listen to and contemplate the teachings and to train in the meditation. The p'howa training itself becomes an arena for actively engaging in bodhichitta through the six perfections of generosity, discipline, patience, perseverance, meditative concentration, and transcendent knowledge. This will be discussed further in the chapter on p'howa training.

The accumulation of merit constitutes the third cause of rebirth in Dewachen, and this is effectively accomplished by performing the Seven-Branch Offering, which is integral to many practices. As it pertains to Amitabha, it consists of the following:

1. Prostrations. Visualizing Buddha Amitabha in the space in front of us, we offer homage to his enlightened form by bringing our hands to the crown of our head, to his enlightened speech by bringing our hands to the throat, and to his enlightened mind by bringing our hands to the heart. Then we make a full-length prostration, visualizing our father on our right, our mother on our left, demons behind us, enemies in front of us, and all beings surrounding us. Everyone prostrates with us, reciting prayers and visualizing Amitabha. One may also visualize countless mental emanations of oneself offering prostrations to

Amitabha. Prostrations antidote the poison of pride.

2. *Offering.* We offer Buddha Amitabha a limitless mandala. The three-thousand-fold universe, representing inanimate phenomena, serves as the container, and all living beings—animate phenomena—are the contents. The offering is arranged as a vast cosmos, with Mt. Meru in the center, surrounded by seven rings of golden mountains jutting up from seas of pure water. At the peak of Mt. Meru are the glorious god realms. In the cardinal directions lie the four continents, each flanked by two subcontinents, including our own southern continent with its wish-fulfilling trees. We visualize goddesses offering pleasurable forms, sounds, scents, things to touch, and foods to taste, as well as the eight auspicious symbols, the seven royal accoutrements, and the eight precious substances—in fact everything that might please by its preciousness, its beauty, or its sacredness. Offering antidotes selfish attachment.

3. *Confession.* Invoking Amitabha as our witness, we acknowledge and express regret for all that we have done wrong through body,

speech, and mind. We vow not to repeat these wrongdoings, and receive Amitabha's purification in the form of light that pervades and completely cleanses us. Confession antidotes anger.

4. *Rejoicing.* By genuinely appreciating and taking pleasure in the virtue of those who pray to and meditate on Amitabha and, more generally, of those who have entered the path to liberation, we antidote the competitiveness and jealousy that sometimes arise toward other dharma practitioners. Whoever sincerely rejoices in the virtue of others accumulates the same merit as the one who accomplishes the virtue.

5. *Requesting teachings.* The accumulation of transcendent knowledge (Tib. *sherab*) is accomplished through hearing, contemplating, and meditating upon the teachings. This begins with a request for the teachings. Specifically, we may request teachings on p'howa and related topics, which antidote our ignorance.

6. *Entreating the victorious ones to remain.* We pray that those who have realization remain accessible to us and not pass into nirvana. By recognizing as inseparable from Buddha Amitabha those lamas who guide us in the meditation

of Amitabha, we cultivate pure perception of what is sacred. This antidotes wrong view.

7. *Dedication.* Meditation on any aspect of Amitabha creates great merit. Offering this merit to the general welfare of beings multiplies it and prevents it from ever being lost or diminished. Through dedication, the virtue generated by an individual increases the virtue of all beings as surely as oil added to a lamp by one person sustains and enhances the light shared by a roomful of people. Dedication antidotes doubts that might arise concerning one's ability to accomplish the ultimate goal of liberating all beings without exception into the great bliss of the pure realm. Dedication is the fourth cause of rebirth in Dewachen.

The Six Bardos

THE EXISTENCE OF BEINGS is conditioned by birth, death, and the transition from death to rebirth. The unceasing arising of karmic forces makes every life form impermanent. We continually cycle through different states of existence, and in p'howa training the most useful way to understand them is within the context of the six bardos, or intermediate states.

The *birthplace bardo* begins at the moment of birth and ends when one meets the irrevocable cause of one's death. It represents one's lifetime, and for human beings it offers a supreme opportunity for spiritual development —the potential to purify negative karma and to gather the accumulations of merit and timeless awareness in order to find liberation from samsara and to lead others to liberation.

The birthplace bardo in the human realm is often textured by two other bardos, the *dream bardo* and the *bardo of meditative concentration* (Skt. *samadhi;* Tib. *samten*). Both of these hold the potential for profound states of consciousness, although for most people they are of very short duration. Like the birthplace bardo, they can be harnessed for spiritual progress.

The dying process takes place in the *bardo of the moment of death,* which closes with the last breath and the merging in the heart chakra of one's original male and female energies. This bardo may be very short-lived, if one meets untimely death by accident or violence, or it may be prolonged, if one dies of a lingering illness. The bardo of the moment of death serves as a crucial transition in the cycle of existence because this is the time when p'howa can be done and liberation into the pure realm easily obtained. However, to accomplish p'howa one should train thoroughly in the practice during the birthplace bardo, because confusion usually prevails at the actual time of death.

For most people the *bardo of the true nature of phenomena* (Tib. *chos nyid* [Skt. *dharmata*] *bardo*) begins when they swoon into blackness after the male and female energies merge in the heart. Very great meditators who are able to maintain awareness throughout the transition of death do not fall into this swoon. During this interval, the mind's qualities are bound into its indestructible essence, into the subtlest core of cognition and motility. The mind's qualities of cognition—the eight aspects of consciousness—are present as the essential sphere (Tib. *t'higle*) of consciousness. The mind's quality of movement is present as extremely subtle karmic energies (or "winds"; Tib. *lung*), which stir the elements of consciousness. This slight stirring dispels the swoon, and the clear light of the true nature of phenomena dawns as an inexpressible, nondual state of unimpeded awareness.

All beings, from any realm of existence, have a momentary experience of clear light when they die, but for most it passes in an instant without being recognized. Only great meditators—those who have realized the highest view through Great Perfection, Mahamudra, or Madhyamika—have the capability of finding liberation into dharmakaya, of attaining enlightenment, through clear light recognition.

For others, liberation is thwarted by a residual urge toward "being" and a fear of annihilation. The subtle aspects of consciousness, further stirred by subtle energies, give rise to the pure phenomena of awareness, the display of the wrathful and peaceful deities. Lights arise, accompanied by thunderous discordant sounds. Then forms emerge from the brilliance, first as the ferocious wrathful deities with their terrifying laughter. Each wears full regalia and is accompanied by a retinue so extensive that it fills space. Then the peaceful deities appear—including the p'howa deities Amitabha, Avalokiteshvara (Tib. Kyanrazig), and Amitayus—resplendent and awesome. Whoever has trained in development stage visualization, who has fully experienced the deity as the display of his or her own mind, may find liberation into sambhogakaya. For others, the display of the peaceful and wrathful deities will flash by. Others will recoil from the relentless radiance, and the visions and sounds of the deities will subside.

Now appears a sequence of four great colored lights, in two intensities each, which mass overhead like an umbrella—first white, then blue-black, yellow, and red. After this sequence manifests, the lights take a variety of shapes.

Then a vision arises like a blueprint of existence, with mandalas of the three kayas and, beneath the mandalas, the six realms of existence. This blueprint is very clear and detailed, and if one recognizes the nature of the three kayas, one gains liberation. If one turns away from the bright lights and is attracted to the dull ones, if one is ignorant of the nature of the three-kaya mandala and is attracted to the six realms, the visions fade and the bardo of the true nature of phenomena ends.

The *bardo of becoming* (Tib. *sidpa bardo*) is like a dream. If one has meditated well enough in one's former lifetime to remember and pray to one's lama or chosen deity, nirmanakaya liberation can still be attained. If one has forgotten one's previous faith or cannot reestablish meditation, great suffering occurs. The bardo of becoming is a desolate place where the sky is a luminous gray, without sun or moon. There is no water or food, and one has all sorts of nightmarish experiences, like being pursued by bands of enemies or wild animals, or falling from mountains as they turn into avalanches. One is immersed in these experiences as though one were in a human body and has no memory of dying, no memory of either the bardo of the moment of death or the bardo of the true nature of phenomena.

One enters the bardo of becoming in a mental body. The energies of the five elements mingle with the subtle aspects of consciousness and the subtle energies of the mental body, making it denser. The five aggregates develop to the point that bardo beings can see and be seen by other bardo beings and by those in other realms with psychic abilities. The sense organs form, and there is need for sustenance, which is taken in the form of smell. Bardo beings never stay long in one place because, in their weightless state, they are instantly carried to whatever their desires touch. At first they might feel a sense of great power and glee in this, but as their desires go here and there and they are compelled to follow, and as these desires are frustrated, bardo beings become increasingly agitated and paranoid. They congregate in old houses, trees, and isolated eerie places, and humans sense them as ghosts.

As the aggregates become denser, the desires, envy, and anger of bardo beings increase. They have visions of beings in the six realms and want what those beings have. The desire to find a form becomes urgent, and this draws them closer and closer to the realm that corresponds to their karmic tendencies. If their consciousness carries murderous anger and hatred, these emotions, full-fledged, become the experience of hell realm rebirth. If craving and miserliness dominate, these tendencies find full projection in the deprived spirit realm. Ignorance and blind instinct lead to embodiment in the animal realm. Jealousy and competitiveness, combined with some measure of virtue, lead to rebirth in the demigod realm, while pride or attachment to meditative bliss, along with virtue, leads to the desire levels of the worldly god realm. Meditation distorted by fixation on clarity—visions, clairvoyance, and so forth—leads to rebirth in the form realms of the worldly gods. Meditation distorted by fixation on stability leads to rebirth in the formless god realm.

Human rebirth results from a combination of merit, gathered through compassionate, loving actions, and nonvirtue, arising from all five poisons. The quality of one's human rebirth—whether one will be rich or poor, well or sick, intelligent or retarded, all of the polarities and the whole spectrum in between—depends precisely on one's individual mix of virtue and nonvirtue. The permutations are countless, because the play of karma is unceasing.

Exhausted by the turbulence of the bardo of becoming, longing for the stability of a body, a bardo being who is destined for human rebirth will be driven toward the sexual union of that being's future parents. If one is to be reborn as a male, there will be attraction to the mother and jealousy toward the father; if one is to be reborn as a female, the attraction will be reversed. At the moment of conception, the substanceless consciousness, propelled by its unceasing subtle energies, merges with the sperm and the egg of the parents. The bardo of becoming continues for about nine months more until birth, which signals that the wheel of samsara has turned a full cycle. Another lifetime begins.

How We Die

HUMAN DEATH FALLS into two categories: death as the natural termination of the life span, whether through sickness or old age, and untimely death by accident or violence. Everyone's death has unique elements according to the circumstances, one's physical condition, and one's state of mind. A general description of the human dying process, however, helps us to comprehend what death is. It is perhaps most helpful to look at this experience from the point of view of the dying person.

In the first stage, the dying person experiences the dissolution of the earth element, sustained in the navel chakra. It becomes impossible to stay erect, to lift one's arms and legs. The head lolls back, the teeth grind, the body appears to shrink. One feels heavy, pressed down. Sight blurs and the eyes stare up unblinking. One is overcome by drowsiness and dullness, a semi-swoon. Though not outwardly apparent, an important secret sign for a meditator is seeing mirage-like visions and flickering lights filling space. A meditator perceives in this the first glimmerings of the unimpeded lucidity on the other side of mind's ordinary obscuration.

In the second stage, the dying person experiences the dissolution of the water element, sustained in the heart chakra. Skin and hair lose their luster, blood and semen coagulate, and one suffers extreme dryness of mouth, nose, throat, and eyes. Bodily sensations are greatly reduced, producing little feeling of pain or pleasure, heat or cold. Hearing diminishes, and ringing and humming in the ears cease. One becomes irritable, uncomfortable, hard to please. The secret sign is seeing visions of smoke filling space.

In the third stage, the dying person experiences the dissolution of the fire element, sustained in the throat chakra. It becomes impossible to swallow, digestion stops completely, inner heat recedes from the limbs toward the center of the body, the exhaled breath becomes colder. The sense of smell fades. One becomes vague, and recognition of even close friends and relatives wavers. The secret sign is seeing visions of red dots like fireflies filling space.

In the fourth stage, the dying person experiences the dissolution of the air element, sustained in the sex chakra. As the sex chakra dissolves, the structure of the body's energy collapses. It becomes impossible to perform any physical actions, the eyes roll back, the voice rasps, respiration is gasping, the senses of taste and touch fail. All aspects of consciousness retract toward the heart chakra. The coarse forms of the vital energies exit, making exhalations protracted.

At this time the karmic energy, which usually abides in the sex chakra, begins to exit. The karmic energy is with one from the moment of conception, and it determines the conditions of one's lifetime. At the moment of death, it sweeps out of the body, giving rise to visionary experiences, a kind of karmic review. Those persons whose activities of body, speech, and mind have been very negative may see terrifying forms or a replay of the bad moments of their lives. They might react with guttural sounds of fear. Those who have been virtuous and kind might experience blissful, heavenly visions and see forms of loving friends and enlightened beings. They will have little fear of death. One no longer has the slightest connection to worldly purposes. The secret sign is seeing flickering butter lamps filling space.

There is one last, long exhalation, followed by the final closure of sight, hearing, smell, taste, and touch. Physically one is dead, but a very subtle process is taking place internally.

Throughout one's life, the essential white drop of energy received from one's father at conception has been sustained in the crown chakra, hanging upside down as a white syllable *Hang*. Now, at the moment of death, it descends through the central channel to the heart chakra, nullifying all concepts related to anger. One experiences a great white illumination like the autumn moon rising.

In the navel chakra, the essential red drop of energy received from one's mother at conception has been sustained in the form of a red syllable *Ah*. Now it rises through the central channel to the heart chakra, nullifying all concepts related to desire. One experiences a great red illumination like the rising sun. (According to another great tradition, the father's white energy is related to desire, the mother's to anger.)

The two drops converge in the heart chakra. Then the subtlest aspects of consciousness, carried by the faintest of energies, subside into the merged drops. All aspects of consciousness related to delusion are nullified. The bardo of the moment of death is over, and one falls into a black swoon like the clear midnight sky. This swoon is the beginning of the bardo of the true nature of phenomena.

What remains of one's being is the indestructible heart drop that holds the bare essence of consciousness and the slightest traces of the vital energies. It may remain in the body for up to three days in an ordinary person, longer in a great meditator. If the deceased is an ordinary person, one should strongly tap the crown of the head right after the last breath to draw the consciousness upward toward the crown chakra and a higher rebirth. Because the consciousness responds to the corpse being touched, one should refrain from handling the body—particularly the feet—to prevent the consciousness from being drawn toward a lower orifice and a lower rebirth. Nor should the body be cremated for three days, lest the consciousness experience being burned. Of course, leaving the body untouched for three days is more difficult in the West than in Tibet.

If p'howa has been successful or other clear signs appear that the consciousness has exited, these restrictions on handling the body do not apply.

P'howa Training

REFUGE AND BODHICHITTA

THE PRAYER OF REFUGE and bodhichitta, repeated three times, opens the p'howa practice. We take refuge in the Three Jewels, recognizing as our guide the Buddha Shakyamuni, who demonstrated perfectly the bodhisattva's path to enlightenment; his dharma teachings as his legacy, our means of following his example; and those who follow him, the sangha, as our companions on the path. We take refuge not just for this lifetime, but until we reach enlightenment, and sustain our bodhichitta intention until not only we, but all beings, reach enlightenment.

To follow the path of the Buddha Shakyamuni, we vow to train constantly in the six perfections of generosity, discipline, patience, perseverance, concentration, and transcendent knowledge. These represent the way of a bodhisattva, one who has vowed to reach enlightenment in order to benefit all beings.

The refuge and bodhichitta prayer, a general prayer also used for other practices, establishes a strong and meaningful foundation for p'howa. It reminds us that the method of p'howa arises from the legacy of the Buddha's teaching and that those who practice with us are the noble sangha. They comprise an exalted category of beings who have looked beyond self-concern, who have seen the suffering of others and have developed the compassionate wish to alleviate it. The blending of this compassionate wish with the aspiration to accomplish it by reaching enlightenment is the birth of bodhichitta and denotes the transformation of ordinary people into sons and daughters of the Buddha.

P'howa training, which is practiced with acute mindfulness of death, provides a powerful arena for actualizing bodhichitta intention. When we contemplate the suffering of dying—the intense uncertainty and the sorrow of severing, one after another, our attachments to friends and family, to wealth, to our personal qualities, to the body itself—do we not break through ordinary concerns? We are inspired to practice both by our fear of death and by our hope that through p'howa we will be able to bypass countless cycles of samsaric rebirth and find direct rebirth in Amitabha's pure realm. Applying the six perfections of the bodhisattva's path to p'howa provides the means to achieve extraordinary powers in this lifetime, including the ability to transfer the consciousnesses of other dying persons. Ultimately, mastering these six trainings leads us not only to the bliss of the pure realm but to full enlightenment.

We express generosity through p'howa by offering our time and effort to train, by learning how to perform p'howa for others, and by our intention to benefit all beings. We cultivate discipline by sitting with good posture and doing each step of the practice well, and by our willingness to put aside outer activities and focus on p'howa during the practice sessions, when others are dying, and at the moment of death. Patience is necessary when we encounter obstacles to practice such as discomfort in sitting and in the process of achieving the physical signs. It is also necessary when others try to hinder us while we are attempting to perform p'howa for the dying or for ourselves. Through perseverance we continue training until we have confidence in our ability and are never dissuaded from pursuing the path that leads to Dewachen. By means of concentration we cut distractions in meditation and constantly bring our attention back to the visualization and recitation. At the moment of dying, we focus on Amitabha, inseparable from our lama.

The perfection of transcendent knowledge occurs through recognition of the practice as a pure manifestation of the union of form and emptiness. The sequence of p'howa meditation brings us to this recognition because in rapid succession we alternate between visualization and dissolution into the nonconceptual, nondual nature of Buddha Amitabha.

MAIN PRACTICE

Visualization of Avalokiteshvara

From the outset of the main body of practice, we break the shackles of ordinary self-perception and bring forth from our essential being the pure manifestation of our nature as Ava-

Avalokiteshvara

lokiteshvara, the Lord of Compassion. Self-visualization as the deity has three important facets: visualizing the image in clear detail, understanding the symbolic meaning of the image, and maintaining the "pride" of the deity—that is, through meditative absorption embodying the body, speech, and mind of the deity without distraction.

To visualize oneself as Avalokiteshvara, rest in the mind's nature as emptiness, holding nothing—not the outer world of sense objects nor the inner world of thoughts, concepts, and emotions. The body is no longer in dense, corporeal form, but rather is luminous, as brilliantly white as a thousand suns shining on a snow mountain. Seated in full vajra posture on a white lotus and moon disk, one has a single face and four arms. The two lower hands clasp a blue wish-fulfilling jewel to the heart; the upper right hand holds a crystal mala and the upper left the stem of a white lotus flower that blossoms near the ear.

As Avalokiteshvara, one wears the five silken garments of the sambhogakaya deities—pendants of five colors hanging from the crown, an upper garment of white silk with golden threads, a long green scarf that winds around and drapes gracefully over the arms, a blue girdle-like short skirt with red pantaloons underneath, and a belt. One also wears the eight jeweled ornaments—a crown with five colored jewels, earrings, three lengths of necklaces, bracelets, armlets, and anklets. These ornaments are elaborately wrought and studded with gems.

Each aspect of the image arises spontaneously and expresses the qualities, the pure display, of absolute nature. In visualizing ourselves as Avalokiteshvara, we are not merely sheathing ourselves in a gorgeous external form. In the nondual realization to which we aspire, all the visual details and their rich meaning unfold naturally from buddha nature, our own and Avalokiteshvara's inseparable.

Avalokiteshvara's brilliant whiteness arises as the quality of being unstained by samsara. His lotus seat is an expression of emptiness, the moon disk skillful means. His single face conveys the unchangeable nature of ultimate truth.

Avalokiteshvara's four arms arise as the display of the four immeasurable qualities of love,

41

compassion, equanimity, and joy. His two hands joined at the heart in the gesture (Skt. *mudra*) of mercy and clasping a blue wish-fulfilling jewel represent love and compassion; the jewel itself brings bliss to beings. His upper right hand holding a mala of equal-sized crystals expresses immeasurable equanimity. His upper left hand holding a lotus that blossoms at the ear conveys immeasurable joy, particularly the joy of hearing the dharma. The stem also bears a fruit and a bud. The fully blossomed flower represents the buddhas of the present; the fruit, the buddhas of the past; and the bud, the buddhas of the future.

The vajra posture is another expression of Avalokiteshvara's immeasurable equanimity, which arises from the absolute realization of the single nature—the single taste, emptiness—of the entirety of samsara and nirvana. His silken garments and jeweled ornaments, worn with utter nonattachment, display the wealth of sambhogakaya. He need abandon nothing because he grasps at nothing.

Visualization of the Central Channel

Exactly in the center of Avalokiteshvara's luminous body is the central channel, running from four finger widths below the navel, where it is closed, to the crown chakra, eight finger widths behind the original hairline, where it is open. It is straight and thin like the shaft of an arrow, soft and flexible like the petals of a lotus flower, and luminous like the light of a butter lamp. Its diameter is that of one's own little finger. It is not a substantial, physical channel, but rather is composed of three concentric shafts of light, the inner one red, the middle one blue, and the outer one white.

The precise centeredness of the channel expresses the great Middle Way, the view that is completely free of the extremes of eternalism (holding to the belief in inherent existence) and nihilism (the belief in no existence, nothingness).

The empty nature of the central channel and its blue shaft correspond to dharmakaya. Its luminosity and the red shaft correspond to the radiant display of sambhogakaya. The function of the channel as the path to the pure realm of

Dewachen and the white shaft correspond to nirmanakaya.

Visualization of the Heart Chakra

In the heart chakra, a luminous membrane of light closes the central channel, so that in meditation we work with only the upper half. Above this luminous membrane an eight-petaled white lotus cups a sphere of shimmering green energy. The eight petals signify the eight aspects of consciousness, which include five aspects associated with the five senses, the aspect that serves as the primordial ground of all ordinary experience, the ideational aspect that allows us to integrate sense data conceptually, and the ego-defiled aspect that gives rise to afflicted emotions.

The shimmering green energy, also described as the "wind of karma," expresses mind's ever-present quality of motility—its ability to go anywhere instantaneously. Cognition, mind's other quality, is embodied in a clear *t'higle* of consciousness that rests lightly on the vibrating green energy. Motility and cognition are interdependent qualities of mind; therefore, the sphere of green energy and the clear *t'higle* of consciousness remain inseparable.

The consciousness *t'higle* is the size of a small pearl and is iridescent with the five wisdom colors—blue, white, red, yellow, and green. The sadhana text refers to it being like "the egg of a masal bird." This simile arose from a glorious vision of the great yogini Machig Lapdron in which she beheld two extraordinary birds in sexual union. Simultaneously each produced from its mouth a jewel-like egg with rings of the five colors. Ordinary mind in its pure nature embodies the five aspects of timeless awareness.

Visualization of Buddha Amitabha

A forearm's distance above one's open crown chakra is Buddha Amitabha inseparable from the lama, seated on a thousand-petaled variegated lotus with a sun disk and moon disk. He is ruby red and radiates brilliant red light in an infinite sphere—his name in Tibetan, Odpagmed, means "boundless light." He possesses the thirty-two major and eighty minor marks of a buddha, including a spherical protrusion at the top of his head, elongated earlobes, a perfectly proportioned body, and eight-spoked chakras on the soles of his feet and on the palms of his hands. As well, he possesses the sixty qualities of enlightened speech, including melodiousness, the ability to project the voice without amplification, and the capacity to communicate without a translator.

In his nirmanakaya form, he wears three special monk's robes, a blue blouse as an inner garment, a yellow upper garment, and an outer robe of red, which correspond to the three trainings of discipline (Skt. *vinaya*), meditative concentration, and transcendent knowledge. His hands, resting in the gesture of meditative equipoise, hold a begging bowl of dark blue lapis lazuli filled with nectar that fulfills the needs and heals the illnesses of beings. He sits in vajra posture.

As with Avalokiteshvara, every aspect of the image holds sacred meaning. The lotus expresses the intrinsic purity of absolute nature that remains unstained by samsaric phenomena. The sun disk corresponds to timeless awareness,

Buddha Amitabha

the moon disk to skillful means. The legs crossed in vajra posture signifies equanimity.

Amitabha's ruby red color arises from his being lord of the lotus (Skt. *padma*) family, with a specific connection to the manifestation of enlightened speech. Through his enlightened intention, Amitabha carries out the activities of power, that is, the activities that draw beings toward liberation through love and discriminating awareness—the simultaneous recognition of the empty nature and manifest detail of all phenomena, as well as the complete interdependence of phenomena.

Visualization of Amitabha's Retinue and the Pure Realm of Dewachen

During p'howa training we may focus on the single figure of Amitabha as our destination, but we should cultivate a sense of his residing in Dewachen, surrounded by a boundless retinue of buddhas and bodhisattvas, the lineage lamas above his head. The bodhisattva Avalokiteshvara stands in two-armed form on a lotus and moon disk to Amitabha's right, his right hand in the gesture of generosity, his left holding the stem of a lotus at his heart. The bodhisattva Vajrapani stands on a lotus and moon disk to Amitabha's left, his right hand facing downward in the gesture of protection, his left holding the stem of a lotus flower that blossoms by his ear. Vajrapani revealed and protects the tantras.

Visualization of Consciousness Transference; the Mantra P'hat

With the recitation of "*P'hat*," the consciousness *t'higle* shoots up from the heart into the heart-mind of Amitabha. This one-syllable mantra contains two sounds. The first is "*p'ha*," which expresses the masculine quality of skillful means; the second is "*ta*," which expresses the feminine quality of wisdom. In the sadhana it is written "*Ah P'hat*." The "*Ah*" is a slight aspirate that is sounded in conjunction with the syllable that precedes it. This means that the first "*Ah*" is attached to the last syllable of the two-line prayer to Amitabha, rendering it "*Lob-Ah*." Then "*P'hay-Ah, P'hay-Ah, P'hat!*"

The sequence of transference begins with establishing the aspects of the visualization—oneself as Avalokiteshvara, the central channel, the consciousness *t'higle* in the heart, Amitabha above. Then we recite the two-line prayer ("I pray to the Buddha Amitabha for the blessing to be born in Dewachen") three times in either Tibetan or English. Focusing strongly on the consciousness *t'higle,* we say "*P'hay-Ah*" and eject the *t'higle* through the channel, through the open crown chakra, and into Amitabha's heart-mind, and then rest in nondual awareness.

Next we focus again on the *t'higle* in our own heart. There is no need to bring the transferred *t'higle* down from Amitabha; we simply refocus, say the mantra, transfer, and rest in nondual awareness.

We repeat the transference a third time—now saying a sharp "*P'hat!*"—and rest. After the third transference, the entire sequence is repeated, beginning with the two-line prayer.

During p'howa training, practitioners may experience some discomfort as the crown chakra opens, perhaps in the form of headaches, dizziness, heat at the top of the head, or a sore spot that may exude a drop of blood or lymph. These are signs of progress and will disappear when the intensity of practice is reduced, although the crown chakra never recloses. We need to train until we are confident that our p'howa path has been established and that we will do p'howa almost automatically at the moment of death. Once we have gained such confidence, we can reduce our training to a single sequence of three prayers and three transferences, and concentrate on the longevity practice instead.

Sometimes people question whether it is safe to train in p'howa, whether one's consciousness might accidentally exit. There is no danger of this. Even when people are weak and verging on death, it often requires great effort to effect the transference. The vital energies bind the mind to the body, and until they decrease enough for the mind to be released, actually transferring one's consciousness is like trying to pull green fruit from a tree: it won't come free until it is ripe.

Lineage Prayer

In p'howa training we do not need to recite the lineage prayer, the prayers for transference to dharmakaya, sambhogakaya, and nirmanakaya, or the prayer to the root lama. However, these prayers are inspiring and refresh our practice with a slightly different focus of visualization.

There are two basic ways to visualize the lineage lamas. The simplest is to visualize them in a single vertical line above the head of Buddha Amitabha in the main visualization, with the dharmakaya aspect of Amitabha at the zenith of the assembly and the other lineage lamas one above another in the same order as in the lineage prayer. Our own root lama sits just above the main visualization of Amitabha.

The second method is to visualize dharmakaya Amitabha sitting at the apex, then slightly below him and to his right Avalokiteshvara in sambhogakaya aspect. The nirmanakaya aspect of Padmasambhava, who brought this p'howa practice into the human realm, sits slightly below Amitabha and to his left. Surrounding these three are all the other lineage lamas, including Padmasambhava's consort, the dakini Yeshe Tsogyal, and his disciple Langdro Konchog Jungnay, whose mindstream emanated as the discoverer of hidden treasure texts (Tib. *terton*) Rigdzin Longsal Nyingpo. Again, our root lama sits amid the assembly, the primary connection for our own liberation.

However we configure the lineage assembly, we experience the profound compassion and powerful realization radiating from each lama, focused on us with the full intention that we find liberation from the endless cycles of life and death. The intention of the lineage lamas connects with our devotion like a hook and eye, uplifting us, drawing us into the pure realm. Steeped in their blessings, we transfer consciousness as before.

Dharmakaya, Sambhogakaya, Nirmanakaya, and Root Lama Prayers

For the dharmakaya prayer, the visualization and transference are exactly as they are after the two-line aspiration prayer to Amitabha. In the transference following the prayer to the sambhogakaya aspect, we visualize either Buddha Amitabha or Avalokiteshvara over our head; if the latter, we as Avalokiteshvara have Avalokiteshvara over our head. Similarly, following the prayer to Padmasambhava as the nirmanakaya aspect, we can visualize either Amitabha or Padmasambhava over our head.

We can likewise perform transference after the prayer to the root lama by visualizing either Amitabha or our root lama above us. "Root lama" refers to the first lama who shows us the nature of mind. Most people do not have a root lama, either because they have not met a qualified teacher or because they have not ripened their receptivity to the lama's direct mind-to-mind transmission. If we do not yet have a root lama, we should visualize Amitabha with the understanding that he embodies all qualities of the enlightened wisdom lama.

Reciting these prayers is like looking at the same essence through different facets of a prism. Our root lama, Guru Padmasambhava, and Avalokiteshvara are inseparable from

Amitabha, arising in different manifestations in response to the specific needs of beings. The intention that we find liberation pulses powerfully through all of them. We need only connect through our own faith and aspiration.

The Longevity Practice
of Amitayus

AT THE CONCLUSION of p'howa practice, Amitabha melts into light and dissolves into us. Instantly, we transform into Amitayus—the buddha of longevity, the sambhogakaya aspect of Buddha Amitabha—who is red and possesses the major and minor marks of an enlightened being. His silken garments and jeweled ornaments are similar to those of Avalokiteshvara. He sits in full vajra posture on a lotus, sun disk, and moon disk. His hands rest in meditative equipoise, and he holds a longevity vase filled with elixir.

In his heart is a locket composed of a moon disk over a sun disk, in the center of which is a red syllable *Hri*. The red syllables of Amitayus's mantra are arranged in a counterclockwise direction on the perimeter of the sun disk, facing outward, evenly spaced. As we recite the mantra, the five lights radiate brilliantly in all ten directions, pervading the pure realms of the buddhas and bodhisattvas, carrying offerings to them. Then light returns as their blessings and is reabsorbed into us as Amitayus. Then, in sequence:

White light radiates and sends offerings to the pure realm of Vairochana, who represents enlightened body. All the blessings of vajra body, form inseparable from emptiness, and of the awareness of the basic space of phenomena (Skt. *dharmadhatu*) emanate from the buddha and are absorbed by us, purifying our grasping at ordinary body, endowing us with the realization of emptiness.

Red light radiates and sends offerings to the pure realm of Amitabha, who represents enlightened speech. All the blessings of vajra speech, sound inseparable from emptiness, and of discriminating awareness emanate from the buddha and are absorbed by us, purifying ordinary perception, fortifying our inner heat.

Blue light radiates and sends offerings to the pure realm of Akshobhya, who represents enlightened mind. All the blessings of vajra mind and of mirror-like awareness emanate from the buddha and are absorbed by us, purifying con-

Amitayus

59

sciousness, fortifying our blood, lymph, and other bodily fluids.

Yellow light radiates and sends offerings to the pure realm of Ratnasambhava, who represents enlightened qualities. All the blessings of vajra qualities and of the awareness of equalness emanate from the buddha and are absorbed by us, purifying feeling, fortifying our skin, bones, and organs.

Green light radiates and sends offerings to the pure realm of Amoghasiddhi, who represents enlightened activities. All the blessings of vajra activities (peaceful, increasing, magnetizing, and wrathful) and of all-accomplishing awareness emanate from the buddha and are absorbed by us, purifying our impulses, fortifying our vital energies.

The mantra lights shine forth again, pervading the entire universe, gathering the essences of the outer elements, which return to dissolve into us and fortify our internal elements. Yellow radiance merges with the precious substances of the earth—gold, jewels, minerals—and gathers essences that dissolve into and revitalize our skin, bones, and organs.

Blue radiance merges with sparkling oceans, waterfalls, and lakes, with the pure liquids of plants, gathering essences that revitalize our blood, lymph, and fluids. Red radiance merges with hot volcanoes and lava flows, with myriad suns, and gathers warmth that revitalizes our inner heat. Green radiance merges with and gathers the essence of air, of the universal winds, which fortifies our own energies. The white radiance arising out of our own empty nature corresponds to the basic space of all phenomena and increases our realization of emptiness.

To conclude the Amitayus longevity practice, we dissolve the visualization and rest in natural, nondual awareness. Then we recite the prayer of aspiration to be born in Dewachen as well as prayers of dedication.

Although the Amitayus longevity practice serves as a section of the p'howa sadhana, one can also perform it independently, opening with prayers of refuge and bodhichitta, concluding with prayers of aspiration and dedication. One establishes the visualization by reciting, "I become Amitayus, emanating light and gathering life's essence, which dissolves into me," then reciting the mantra.

The emphasis in p'howa shifts to Amitayus longevity practice after we have attained good signs of transference. We should practice it whenever our elements are weak or out of balance, or when our life force has diminished. We can also do the practice as a means of healing others by visualizing that the blessings and elemental essences dissolve into them. Practice based on this kind of compassionate intention purifies the practitioner as well and generates tremendous merit, both of which are the causes of good health in the future.

P'howa as a Daily Meditation

WHEN THE GREAT mahasiddha Kumaraja was about to leave his body, he invited all his disciples to come and sit around him in a circle. At the moment he sounded a single "*P'hat!*" his consciousness shot out of the central channel through his crown chakra and rainbow lights filled the sky in all directions.

When the Chinese Communists took over Tibet, they were very ruthless, particularly before they consolidated their political power. Many monks and yogis were tortured and killed, but some who were p'howa masters transferred their consciousness before the Chinese could take their lives. They did so not as a suicidal escape, but to spare the Chinese the immense negative karma of killing.

A person who has truly mastered p'howa need not fear death or any circumstances of death, including pain, violence, or suddenness. But mastery depends on more than having opened the channel and the power of visual-

63

ization. It depends on having cut through clinging to the illusions of samsara—one's body, possessions and endowments, and loved ones. This cannot be overemphasized, because attachment is the great obstacle to obtaining liberation through p'howa.

Rather than abandoning the objects of attachment, we must decrease attachment itself by constantly reestablishing the view that nothing has inherent existence. If we examine anything, we will at least recognize that it is transitory, changing instant by instant. If we examine it to an infinitesimal degree, we will find it is empty, only a possibility.

Holding the view of emptiness is not an excuse for indifference or apathy. Rather, it gives us reason to open to each experience as it arises, without grasping or pushing away. If we deeply contemplate impermanence and emptiness, and are able to establish this view in all types of situations, life's inner significance unfolds. If we are well established in view, we are prepared to die without regret.

Death is life's most awesome event, and as a rehearsal of this event, p'howa practice has unique power as a method for training the mind. When we wake in the morning, we should pause and think, "I'm alive. That is a great thing. Now I have another day in this useful human body to develop the positive qualities of my mind. Or at least I won't cause harm by creating anger."

During the day, we are mindful of body, speech, and mind. As p'howa practitioners, we should frequently visualize Buddha Amitabha, inseparable from our lama, above the crown chakra and offer a silent prayer to be born in Dewachen. We can do this anytime, while performing other activities.

If we wish to devote the body to spiritual practices, we might perform prostrations, circumambulate sacred shrines, practice yogic postures to stabilize meditation, or work in service to others. The spiritual uses of speech include chanting sadhanas and reciting mantra, and speaking as a means of communicating compassion. Mind is our foundation and is worth careful observation. What is surfacing? Are obsessive thoughts revolving around poisonous emotions? Are endless concepts filling all the spaces? What motivates our mental processes?

To observe the mind and train it, we must meditate. By entering the bardo of meditative concentration, we find the nature of samsaric phenomena revealed as pure display, the manifestation of the deity's form, speech, and mind. Momentarily the mind's dualistic processes cease and we can directly experience phenomena inseparable from their empty nature.

The birthplace bardo and the dream bardo are similar in their illusory nature. By cultivating recognition of the dreamlike quality of waking life, by cultivating meditation in our dreams, we can penetrate the seeming reality of each state and free the mind's attachment to illusory appearance.

As p'howa practitioners, we should look back each night and reflect on our day. If we were to die in the night, would we be satisfied with the accomplishments of this last day? If we have been involved in negativity, we pray to be purified using the four powers of enlightened witness, remorse, commitment not to repeat our negative actions, and purification by light or nectar. If we have created some merit through virtuous activities, we rejoice in having had this opportunity. Nothing is ever lost in the karmic equation. Even a single kind act like feeding a hungry dog or bird has significance and multiplicity, and will be the cause of better conditions in the future. To actively multiply such merit, we dedicate it to the welfare of all beings. Like a raindrop dissolving in the ocean, the benefit expands and will never diminish.

Having reflected on the day in this way, we contemplate our death. We imagine different scenarios: an automobile accident, cancer, attack by a knife-wielding mugger, a gunshot. We make our drama so vivid that real anxiety arises in our mind. After all, none of us knows how we will die, or when. All possibilities remain out there, on the periphery of our existence, and one of them will definitely surface according to our karma.

Confidence comes from having p'howa as a method. Even as we imagine our painful separation from friends and family, the heaviness of body, and the last gasping breaths, we experience peace at a deeper level and devotion to our lama inseparable from Amitabha. We long for union and feel joy at the prospect of continuing our path in Dewachen. Within this framework, we do several sequences of transference, some longevity practice if we choose, we dedicate, and then we sleep.

Accomplishing P'howa
at the Moment of Death

THE PROCESS OF DYING slowly from a prolonged illness or old age often involves many cycles of nearing death and recovering. In this situation, we must negotiate extreme fluctuations of hope and fear by continually contemplating impermanence. Knowing that no situation—nothing whatsoever—remains stable or lasting, we free ourselves from the frustration of trying to stabilize conditions. We observe the dreamlike quality of everything that arises and relax within the arising. In this state of open awareness, we can more easily recognize when the time to die has come, and we have less resistance to this knowledge.

We will know that no more medicines, no more prayers will avert our death. Out of respect for precious human existence, we will have done what we could to preserve our life, but now we are going to leave our body and the lifetime that provides its context. We are ready for the final preparations for death.

If we are able, we should give away our possessions. A formal, written will has immense value because it allows us to direct our material wealth to the highest benefit. This gesture of generosity frees us from attachment to what we cannot hold anyway and creates merit.

Likewise, if we are capable and have not already done so, we should write a "living will" regarding which resuscitation techniques and life-sustaining medical procedures are acceptable to us and which we want to avoid. If possible, this should be a formal legal document backed up by another that assigns "durable power of attorney" to someone we would trust to carry out our wishes and make our medical decisions were we to fall into a coma or become otherwise incapacitated.

Also useful and deeply appreciated is a letter informing our friends and family about which practices, including p'howa, should be performed and explaining how they can assist us in dying and after death. An example of such a letter can be found in the Appendixes.

As we approach death, we review for the last time our karma of body, speech, and mind. We review our commitments as spiritual practitioners, our sacred words of honor, and the promises we made to our lama. We invoke Amitabha—or any other enlightened being—inseparable from our lama, as our witness. We confess to any nonvirtue we have created, especially intentional harm, and our failures to keep commitments. Through absolute honesty with ourselves, we generate genuine remorse. Making a commitment never to repeat such downfalls in future lifetimes, we receive absolution from our enlightened witness, by light or nectar or both.

Now we summon all of the virtue, material wealth, and positive qualities of all our lifetimes and create a glorious and extensive mandala offering to the buddhas and bodhisattvas of the ten directions. The virtue of this offering is then dedicated to all beings.

Only we can gauge our internal processes of bodily dissolution, and we should be particularly mindful of the sequence of secret signs—mirages, smoke, sparks like fireflies, and lights like butter lamps. These indicate that the veil between our present condition and the illumination of the bardo of the true nature of phenomena is becoming thinner. When the breath is short, the body is heavy and chilled, and the sense impressions are vague, we ask our friends to prop us erect if possible. If not, they should roll us on our right side in lion posture, the posture in which Buddha Shakyamuni passed into parinirvana. Then, if our friends are not p'howa practitioners or have not been told what to do, it would be better if they left. Of course, this is not always possible, but at least they should not distract us.

Alone now, we should have no fear. We have died countless times before, and this time we have refuge and a powerful spiritual method. We have rehearsed this moment through our p'howa training. We block our nine openings (soles of the feet, two lower orifices, mouth, nostrils, ears) with visualized seed syllable *Hungs*. Our mind joyously turns toward Dewachen and Buddha Amitabha. Even if our visualization is vague, we know that Amitabha, inseparable from our own lama, is present above the crown of the head. We yearn to join our lama. Then we focus on the consciousness *t'higle* as strongly as possible.

Saying "*P'hat!*" again and again, we shoot the *t'higle* out of the crown, performing each ejection with concentration and force as if it were our last. Now the final strong exhalation is coming. We concentrate all our remaining power into this ejection, completing the separation of mind and body. Union with Buddha Amitabha is nondual; it is liberation into the pure realm.

LIBERATION WHEN THE PRACTITIONER CANNOT PERFORM P'HOWA

If death comes suddenly and there is no time to perform p'howa, or if one is incapacitated, p'howa training can still bring about liberation, first in the clear light phase of the bardo of the true nature of phenomena. This state of unimpeded awareness corresponds to the natural, nondual awareness experienced in meditation after transference of consciousness into the heart-mind of Amitabha. If this state has been stabilized in meditation, it is possible to attain dharmakaya liberation after death.

The pure display of sambhogakaya represents a second opportunity for liberation. Training in p'howa familiarizes one with the pure appearance of Avalokiteshvara, Amitabha, and Amitayus. Particularly, experiencing one's nature as Avalokiteshvara in meditation enables one to recognize the spontaneous appearance of Avalokiteshvara in the bardo of the true nature of phenomena as none other than the display of one's own nature. This recognition brings about sambhogakaya liberation.

A third opportunity for liberation arises in the bardo of becoming. Upon realizing one has died, and as the tumultuous sights and sounds and emotions gather force, if one has a strong habit of prayer, one might pray to Amitabha. Having only an insubstantial bardo body, one will be propelled to whatever the mind touches, including Amitabha. This will bring about nirmanakaya liberation.

PERFORMING THE P'HOWA
OF THE COMPASSIONATE HOOK

The first thing to do when someone dies is to forcefully tap the top of the person's head. This directs the consciousness upward. A p'howa practitioner who has achieved good signs may then transfer the deceased's consciousness. This is accomplished by visualizing oneself as Avalokiteshvara and the deceased as Avalokiteshvara seated in vajra posture above the prone corpse. One visualizes a stream of green energy shooting from one's heart to the heart of the deceased, where it strengthens the vibration of his or her energy. The two-line prayer to Amitabha and three mantric "*P'hats*" are recited just as in the training. However, total attention is given to the transference of the dead person's consciousness into the heart-mind of Amitabha.

Recognition that Avalokiteshvara embodies the essence of the deceased enables one to accomplish the transference. The corpse is merely an illusion, a temporary dwelling place; Avalokiteshvara is a pure appearance arising from the indestructible nature of the deceased's mind. Experiencing this directly in meditation frees one from the dichotomy of corpse and visualization.

The p'howa practice can be done silently, especially if it would offend relatives and or create a disturbance in the hospital. Some hospitals are sympathetic to requests for time alone with the corpse, particularly if arrangements have been made ahead of time. If the dying person is a practitioner and has asked us to support his or her p'howa practice with our own, it is preferable to perform it aloud. If, however, the person has a resistance to death and if p'howa would increase his or her agitation and fear, it is better to refrain from doing it. It can be performed after the person has died. It is always of primary importance not to antagonize or distress the dying person. Conflict with family and caretakers should be avoided; tact and flexibility are essential.

P'howa can be performed for non-Buddhists, but if they have not received initiation and training, it is inappropriate to teach them without authorization from a qualified lama. We may suggest that they visualize their own object of spiritual refuge above their head. However, while performing p'howa on their behalf, we should maintain the visualization of Amitabha rather than a substitute based on their tradition. If they have an aversion to Buddhism, we do not perform p'howa at all. Instead, we offer general prayers and dedicate the merit of any personal practice to them.

Sometimes many repetitions are required before the signs of successful transference appear on the crown of the head. These include a swelling, a patch of easily plucked hair, or a drop of blood or lymph. Milarepa once sat by the side of the road for a week performing p'howa on the corpse of a dog. Should we expect to spend only a few minutes practicing on behalf of someone we care about? If they cannot rely on us to take whatever time is necessary, who can they rely on?

Until the signs are clear, it is best not to touch the body except to rap the head. Afterward, it does not matter whether the corpse is cremated or buried.

PERFORMING P'HOWA FOR ANIMALS

Because the craniums of animals are structurally different from those of humans, it is not possible to create the same kind of opening in the crown chakra. Therefore, instead of sending the green energy to the animal's heart, one draws its consciousness *t'higle* into one's heart and merges it with one's own consciousness, transferring it out of one's crown chakra into Amitabha's heart-mind. It is not easy to transfer the consciousness of animals, so many people sponsor recitations of the Buddha Akshobhya's mantra and the creation of an image of him for animals they are deeply concerned about. Akshobhya practice is particularly effective because he established as his intention that whoever recited one hundred thousand recitations of his mantra and created an image of him would be released from rebirth in the lower realms. However, performing any practice and dedicating the merit to a deceased animal creates benefit.

Aspiration Prayer and Dedication

THE TREASURE TEXT OF Rigdzin Longsal Nyingpo closes with an aspiration prayer to accomplish p'howa, to be reborn in Dewachen without other rebirths intervening and see the face of Buddha Amitabha directly. It does not include a specific dedication prayer. H.E. Chagdud Rinpoche suggests using the dedication from the concise Red Tara sadhana practiced at Chagdud Gonpa centers. The dedication he wrote for a *sur* practice (the offering of nourishing scents) is also appropriate. Both prayers are included in the Appendixes.

Whichever prayers of dedication we choose to recite, we should offer the virtue and merit of our p'howa practice expansively.

To those who have been ushered into the bardo of the moment of death by disease: by cancer, AIDS, hepatitis, tuberculosis, malnutrition, or malaria; by the deterioration of their hearts, lungs, or brains; by the whole array of illnesses that afflict beings:

May the confusion inflicted by disease give way to clarity. May their illnesses purify whatever negative karma remains in their mindstreams. May compassion for others in similar situations arise in their hearts. May they find liberation into the pure realm at death, and thereafter ultimate liberation.

To the elderly, whose vital forces are ebbing away, leaving them exhausted; whose resources of friends and family are dwindling, leaving them isolated and lonely; whose sensory and mental capacities are diminishing, leaving them uncertain and bewildered; whose joys and accomplishments are fading into vague memories, leaving them sad and vulnerable:

May they recognize the illusion of their corporeal form and slip from its sheath smoothly. May they find the spiritual support to cross the threshold of death with confidence. May they find liberation from suffering and ultimate enlightenment.

To those who die suddenly or by violence, and who are subject to panic and almost uncontrollable anger:

By the merit of whatever good karma they have generated in all of their lifetimes, by the merit of our prayers and practice, may they find protection and release from the trajectory of those last, awful moments. May peace dawn in their mindstreams, may they find liberation from all fear and suffering. May they attain enlightenment.

To those who have died inauspiciously in the past and found rebirth in states devoid of leisure to practice:
By the merit of our prayers and practice, may they find liberation from their own mind's projections and rest in the unimpeded awareness that is enlightenment.

To those who have trained in p'howa, who know the method but are hindered by attachments and uncertainty about when to perform p'howa:
May they recognize the illusory nature of their attachments; may they overcome all hesitation through the power of awareness. May the dedication of our prayers and practice merge with their own skillful means and wisdom, and may

transference into the pure realm be swift and sure. May they reach enlightenment quickly, to benefit all beings.

To the holy lineage lamas:
Through our merit, may their longevity be strengthened, their activities flourish, and their blessings—the extraordinary bridge between this human realm and the pure realm—be sustained through the practice of p'howa.

Appendixes

EXAMPLE OF A
LETTER OF INSTRUCTION

TO MY MUCH LOVED family and friends, instructions for the time of my death:

First of all, I want you to know how deeply I care for you. Our connection in this lifetime, especially our moments of affection and happiness, represent my great good fortune. The process of dying brings home powerfully the realization that, as surely as we have come together, we must separate and the time in between is all too brief. Of course I feel sorrow, but I also feel a sweet and intense appreciation of what we have shared.

As death approaches, however, any ordinary attachment I have for you will not help, since I am powerless to turn back from this journey. And your attachment to me, though very natural, will not be useful because it may distract me and turn my attention to where I cannot really return—back to the circumstances of my life with you—and hinder me in the tricky transition of death. What I need from you now is calmness, release, and the recognition that however my death appears outwardly, inwardly it is a profound spiritual opportunity. Your prayers, arising from your own depths of love and compassion, will certainly support me in my efforts to use this opportunity well.

You know that my spiritual training in recent years has been in Tibetan Vajrayana Buddhism. The lineage masters of this tradition have left clear descriptions of what occurs at death and what meditational skills are needed to negotiate death's transition. Specifically, I have learned a technique called p'howa, or transference of consciousness at the moment of death. I have asked some Buddhist practitioners to be present at my death and assist me in the practice. They will help me sit up, if possible, and they will do the practice with me. They may also tap the top of my head, since the purpose of p'howa is to direct the consciousness out of the crown of the head toward a destination of spiritual rebirth. P'howa does not involve any flamboyant ritual, and it does not take more than an hour or so.

Hospitals are usually very willing to create space and time for this meditation, especially if you discuss it with the staff ahead of time.

What follows is a checklist of instructions. I hope they are clear, because I may not be able to clarify them when I am closer to death, but you may ask any of my lamas or dharma friends on the list below if you have questions.

1. Please notify my lama and dharma friends in time for them to be present before I die. Of course, it may be hard to tell when the actual moment of death will occur; if it somehow happens that they can't arrive in time, don't worry. The blessings of my spiritual training will support my passing.

2. Please do not touch my body, particularly my hands or feet, as death approaches because your loving contact may draw my attention downward when my whole focus should be at the crown of my head.

3. If no other spiritual practitioner is present when I die, tap my skull in the center about eight finger widths back from my original hairline. This could be of immense benefit in channeling the exit of my consciousness.

4. It is best if my body is not handled much before the p'howa practice is finished. Certain signs occur when transference is successful, which other practitioners will recognize. When the practice has been successful, it doesn't matter at all what happens to my corpse. I would prefer it to be cremated as inexpensively as possible and the ashes used in the making of *tza-tsas,* small sacred images stamped out of clay. A lama can instruct you. If *tza-tsas* prove too difficult to make, just have my dharma friends scatter the ashes and offer prayers. They are only ashes, the merest residue of my life.

5. I am an organ donor, and hopefully my consciousness will be transferred before anyone comes to harvest my organs. It not, don't worry: my lama assures me that the mere offering of organs supersedes the disturbance to the body and my consciousness will be directed to a high state of rebirth on the basis of that merit.

6. There is a slight possibility that transference won't be achieved, my organs won't be harvested, and my consciousness will remain lodged in my body for up to four days and three nights. This will cause difficulties for you,

because my body should definitely not be buried or cremated until the consciousness has exited—a lama can check to see if it has done so. In California and other states, you can keep the body as long as you have a death certificate and the body is properly refrigerated, but you can't bury or cremate it yourself. I don't want to burden you with my dead body (forgive me if many humorous possibilities spring to mind), but I want you to at least know about not destroying it prematurely. If you can't find a place to let it rest, then call the lamas and my dharma friends and urge them to practice p'howa. Performing p'howa successfully from a distance requires a very great meditator, so it would be best if they did the practice next to the body.

7. Please make offerings to the lamas who perform prayers and ceremonies after my death. I have designated a certain amount of money in my will for this purpose. I know I have not been the most virtuous person in this lifetime, and unless p'howa is successful and I take rebirth in a state beyond suffering and can purify my misdeeds there, I may be confronted after death with the full weight of my negative actions of

body, speech, and mind. This will definitely cause me suffering. You can alleviate this by asking my dharma friends to arrange for prayers to be said and for ceremonies to be conducted. Particularly, I want to sponsor a practitioner to recite the Akshobhya mantra and to create an image of that buddha. This will cost about $130 and can be facilitated through the Mahakaruna Foundation at P.O. Box 344, Junction City, CA 96048; (530) 623-2302. My lamas will suggest other ceremonies. A list of lamas and dharma friends appears below.

Thank you for all that you have done and will do. I know that it requires a certain tolerance to honor my spiritual belief system when it is different from your own, but I can hope that your respect for my requests will become a source of positive energy that will ease your mind at the time of your own death. According to the teachings I have received, if all goes well, after death I will find liberation from selfish concerns in the realms beyond death and will attain vastly enhanced abilities to benefit you and all beings. This is what I most wish. May it come about just so!

DEDICATION PRAYER FROM AN AVALOKITESHVARA SUR OFFERING

This virtuous accumulation of merit we offer so that all obstacles dissolve, and that at the time of our death, each of us may find ease in dying and swift rebirth in the pure realm of Great Bliss, quickly gaining enlightenment for the benefit of all sentient beings.

PRAYERS FROM THE CONCISE RED TARA PRACTICE

Dedication Prayer

Throughout my many lives and until this moment, whatever virtue I have accomplished, including the merit generated by this practice and all that I will ever attain, this I offer for the welfare of sentient beings.

May sickness, war, famine, and suffering be decreased for every being, while their wisdom and compassion increase in this and every future life.

May I clearly perceive all experiences to be as insubstantial as the dream fabric of the night and instantly awaken to perceive the pure wisdom display in the arising of every phenomenon.

May I quickly attain enlightenment in order to work ceaselessly for the liberation of all sentient beings.

Prayer of Aspiration

Buddhas and bodhisattvas altogether: whatever kind of motivation you have, whatever kind of beneficial action, whatever kind of wishing prayers, whatever kind of omniscience, whatever kind of life accomplishment, whatever kind of benevolent power, and whatever kind of immense wisdom you have, then similarly I, who have come in the same way to benefit beings, pray to attain these qualities.

The Auspicious Wish

At this very moment, for the peoples and the nations of the earth, may not even the names disease, famine, war, and suffering be heard. Rather may their moral conduct, merit, wealth, and prosperity increase, and my supreme good fortune and well-being always arise for them.